# POETIC RIDDLES:

# ACROSTICS

Are you able?
Can it be done?
Rest on laurels,
Old age you've won.
Stagnant, be not,
Try a new way.
Inactive's bad,
Charge up the day.
Savor God's way!

R. A. GILMORE

ISBN: 979-8-9872766-6-2

# Table of Contents

# Preface

God is the inspiration for the writing of the poems, with the delightful and gracious Holy Spirit leading the process. Learning to be patient and yielding to the Holy Spirit's leading is a joyfully blessed and challenging adventure of growing in faith. The Lord has encouraged and guided this opportunity to work with Him. His hand provides what results as these writings.

The scriptures cited are from the New American Standard Bible, copyright 1971, 1995, 2020. Some other translations are used occasionally and those translations are cited when used.

Though I put the pen to the paper, the pen is guided by the Holy Spirit working through me. I bear the responsibility for the written words and accept the burden of any and all errors. All the honor and glory is to go to God.

While the three-word title of this book may seem a bit strange, there is rationale behind it. The Bible contains many poems, yet the word "poem" is not found in the Biblical text. The word "riddle" is found in several places in the Bible (Judges 14:12-19; 1Kings 10:1; 2 Chronicles 9:1; Psalm 49:4; Psalm78:2; Proverbs 1:6; Ezekiel 11:2; Ezekiel 20:49; Daniel 5:12). The word "acrostic" is not found in the Biblical text, however, there are many acrostics in the Bible (see the Introduction). Thus, each of the three words in the title have direct connection to the Bible.

I trust this collection of poems will be helpful to the reader and will be an enjoyable venture that draws you closer to God as you walk with the Lord. Perhaps some will provide new insights into your understanding of God's written Word.

God is the poet,
I am the recording secretary.

R. A. Gilmore

# Foreword

In 1970, when I first met Richard Gilmore, it was clear that he was a faithful man of The Church, following in the steps of our generous Savior. My wife, infant son, and I had no place to stay, and Dr. Gilmore, busy though he was at Southern Illinois University, took the time and expense to provide us with housing. Since then, he has been a confidant and friend, not just to me, but serving many others in many ways as he serves Christ. He still is at that glorious task.

His contribution to us now is in poetry, through which he demonstrates an amazing propensity toward creativity that blesses all who read his lines, and opens the reader's mind to higher growth. Richard Gilmore surely contributes to us a deeper faith.

I visited his home a year or so after he became a widower, having lost his wonderful, caring wife, Janine. He was still a family man, with on-going relationships with his three children. His creativity was evident in woodwork. Here is an active, ingenuitive man who does not quit and will not until God takes him Home.

It is a joy and privilege to recommend this fine book of poetry of double art, poems that employ not only rhyme according to theme, but also acrostic meaning. The reader will look far to find this type of poetry, beyond this book. Here you have it already! His introduction also includes a fascinating

exposition of acrostic poetry . . . . . .
written by a servant who keeps on serving.

J. Wyatt George

Assistant Pastor for Missions
Grace Presbyterian Church (PCA)
Carbondale, IL.

Executive Secretary of The TentMaker Project, an economic development mission in Uganda, East Africa.

Author, husband, married for 57 years, and father of four sons, one in church ministry, one in military chaplaincy, and two in construction trades.

# Introduction

What is an acrostic? Technically it is a puzzle. It is a literary device in the form of a puzzle to reveal and to hide. The different appearances could be words or letters, but any sequence could be the building block to form the acrostic.

Resorting to dictionaries for the definition may prove fruitless since some dictionaries do not have the word "acrostic" in their lexicon (1957 *A Dictionary of Contemporary American Usage*; 1944 *The Westminster Dictionary of the Bible*; 1978 *Webster's School and Office Dictionary*). Probably the best definition is found in the 1967 *The New Compact Bible Dictionary*, and it is basically the following: acrostic is a literary modality generally found in poetry. The first letter of each line of the poem forms a word or phrase or a consecutive sequence of letters of the alphabet.

Acrostics have a storied and lengthy history. Acrostics have been around since the ancient Greeks. Evidence of early writers producing acrostics have been discovered in the writings of Renaissance authors in Italy and Germany. Acrostics are found in the Bible and these include Psalms 9-10, 25, 34, 37, 111, 112, 119, and 145. Psalm 119, a frequently cited example of the acrostic, has successive groups of eight verses where each line of the group of eight starts with the same letter of the Hebrew alphabet. Working through the Psalm will take you, in order, through the 22 letters of the Hebrew alphabet. One important fact is that the English translation of the

Hebrew poem does not reflect this sequence. Some English translations will have the Hebrew letter indicated at the beginning of each of the set of eight lines. Other Biblical acrostics are found in Proverbs, Lamentations and Nahum.

Typically, the acrostic is the first letter of each line of a poem, but that is not a requirement. It probably is the easiest to construct. Other schemes have been used by poets, some almost hidden to the casual reader. An example of this is the Edgar Allen Poe poem titled *A Valentine*. The acrostic will be left for you to discern. With the exception of Biblical authors, Poe and Lewis Carroll are probably the most prolific acrostic writers.

For acrostic poems, the word or phrase in the acrostic may or may not be related to the content of the poem. The purpose or intent of the acrostic is to make known while attempting to hide within the poem.

Some acrostics may have the word, or sequence, as a familiar word from languages other than English. These may include Aramaic (Hebrew), Greek, or Latin. Bible students would recognize the words and their definition.

Most acrostics are formed from reading down the first letter of each line of the poem. There are some acrostics that use only parts of the poem. Other acrostics may be based on reading the letters from bottom to top. Some acrostics may be repeats for each stanza. Thus, for any combination you can conjure, you could make it the puzzle for the acrostic.

This collection of poems is a sampling of what one can do with the poem, both in the poem titles and the acrostic puzzle. The more complex the puzzle, the more difficult the construction.

Perhaps these poems will give you a challenge in reading and a surprise in the puzzle. Remember, there are no defined limits to the way the poem and the acrostic intersect.

# Poems

## Good News

Growing in Christ, our risen Lord,
Open to receive His great Word.
Seeking to live out God's own will,
Pressing on, His love to fulfill.
Excited with all He does send,
Living in Him throughout the end.

## Precedence

Purveying my list of things to do,
Racing the press of time,
I shudder at trying to figure out
Only what is sublime.
Realizing there is only one way,
It makes life worthwhile,
To know that I can face each day,
Yes, Jesus is my smile.

## Grin

Smirks can brighten up a room,
Making bright what once was gloom.
Infectious at times they will be,
Letting all become happy.
Encourage those all around,
So grins will much more abound.

## Guide

Joy and comfort He does provide.
Every step He's at my side.
Sustains me and even does chide.
Unwavering and loving guide.
Shelters me, in Him I abide.

(Father's Day)
(Written at Tulip Grove Baptist Church, Old Hickory, TN)

# Intercession

Taking time, for others to pray
Helps them and also helps you
Enhancing each throughout the day.

Lifting up others to the Lord
Opens our heart to hear God's Word,
Reinforces our walk with Christ.
Develops a Christ-like habit,
Strengthens our desires to not quit.

Perseverance is the main key
Restoring others unto Thee.
Adding more substance to their life,
Yielding self to reduce their strife.
Encouragement for them and you
Reaps much grace and grows a God-
view.

# Praise, Adoration and Glory to God

Adoration should go to God.
Blessing God is such a delight.
Confessing to God honors Him,
Delivers our soul from our plight.

Extoling God strengthens our walk.
Faith does keep us on the path true.
Gospel readings strengthen the heart.
Honoring God's the thing to do.

Image of God is how we were made.
Jesus is our Savior and Lord.
Kneel in humble obedience.
Laved by knowing God's written word.

Mighty miracles God performs.
Noteworthy acclaim God has earned.
Omniscient is one of God's traits.
Promises fulfilled we have learned.
Quietly yielding hearts to God,
Righteous living God's never spurned.

Sabbath observance God does love.
Tribute to God we ever bring.
United with Christ through God's will.
Veneration to God we sing.

Wisdom does come from God alone.
Xenial is what we should be.
Yielded to Christ will bring us life.
Zealous for Christ will set us free.

# Valentine's Day

Always ready to celebrate
Donning party hats on our pate.
Actively being so involved
Yet wanting hearts to be resolved.
Tenderness towards others does count
Opening hearts as joy does mount.
Heaping joy on all those around,
Offering love that does abound,
Nourishing hope that is profound.
Open hearts that readily sing
Resounding joy to others bring.
Let sweet love flow free from your
heart
Opening a new way to start.
Valiant love should be on display
Ev'rywhere on Valentine's Day.

# Tintinnabulation

Tolling of bells we rarely hear
Harking thus to mortal travail.
Remember not the carillon
Echoing o'er the hill and dale?
Ever that music does remain
Near and dear to our ageing heart.
Above all odds those sounds endure,
Inviting memories to start,
Lingering greatly in our mind,
Savoring memories it does impart.

# Seeking

Remember the patriarchs of old.
Each was sought by a love that was
bold.
An offer was made from God's own
hand,
Calling them unto that Promised Land.
Hear that voice calling for you and me
Into a life so full and so free.
Now is the best time to heed that call.
God is still seeking – seeking for all.

# Delight

Call it what ever you think,
Heavenly is what to cry.
Often it's the staff of life
'Cause it e'er will satisfy.
Occasional 'twill bring strife.
Leaving it, not an option.
Always take it is the plan
To every place you might go.
Eat all the sweetness you can.

(Written while on the Norwegian Star cruise ship sailing to Vancouver)

## Quest

Seeking life's gusto I took all of its
thrills,
Eagerly yielding, yet suffering great
spills.
At last realizing it just wouldn't work,
Repenting, I turned my life with a jerk.
Coming to Christ was the opening of
joy,
His Spirit now has my life to employ.

# Equipping the Saints

Disciplined learning takes each
moment of life
Invested in God, whether joy or strife.
Seeing Him in all that you do
Changes the way that you will view
Interaction with others along the way –
People with whom you work and play.
Leaning on Him allows you to be
Examples of love to all that you see.
Setting God as priority one
Honors the Father and the Son,
Instilling in you the way to grow,
Provides you strength as through life
you go.

## Color Tints

Surveying the vast and glorious view,
Portrayed in various color and hue,
Reminds me this marvelous scene so
grand
Indeed was painted by God's loving
hand.
Notice the colors, the tones, and the
shade,
Green colors so varied as they parade,
Touting their different tones all around.
In awe, one wants to stand here on this
ground.
Many the green spot, so deep and so
dark,
Edged by yellow-green quite bright and
quite stark.

Hues do change from vivid brilliant to
dull
Under the clouds that are puffy and
full.
Exquisite, unique, this color display –
Springtime's new life is again in full
sway.

(Based on the scenery seen while driving from
Hugo, OK to Tulsa, OK)

## Attitude

Skittering about like a bunch of bugs,
Trailing the crowd as if we were thugs,
Actions like these do not fill our mugs.
Noticing needs are our spark plugs.
Doing good deeds instead of drugs.

Seeking the comfort of the crowd,
Taking whatever they deem proud,
Alerts me with a signal loud,
Now it's time for that which is vowed,
Deeds of good is the field I plowed.

Students have banded together today
Taking a stance that is tough to play.
Actions for good is now what they say,
Not those things that lead to dismay.
Drugs and such things are now passe.

# Plaudits

Plaudits we offer unto Thee
Ringing out ever joyously.
Adoration is Thine alone
Immortal God upon Your throne.
Singing from the depths of our heart,
Enjoying grace you do impart,
Honor we do give unto You.
Only Your will we try to do,
Needing Your love each passing day,
Owing love to those on the way.
Reaping the joy of Your great love,
Glory to God in heav'n above.
Love is all that You ask indeed,
Offering help in time of need.
Remaining at our side each day
You do guide us along our way.

(Written while flying from Tulsa, OK, to
Washington, D.C.)

# Pardoned

Foraging on God's Word daily,
Observing all that it does say.
Remembering Christ died for all,
Giving all that I have today.
Investing in service for others,
Venturing Christ's path for my life.
Encouraging others in Christ,
Needing Christ to handle my strife.

(Written while on the Norwegian Star cruise ship sailing to Vancouver)

## Our Image

Keeping up our valued image,
Overlooking our own short-falls,
Is an invitation to failure,
Nailing our theses to the walls.
Our God will set aside some things,
Never, never holding a grudge.
In detail God knows all our heart
And still loves us, gives us a nudge.

## The Event

Preparation's always helpful,
Anticipation is not dull.
Readiness gets you on the track,
Obeisance helps you not be slack.
Understanding will serve you well,
Seeking the time, there do not dwell.
It will only occur one time,
Action will be there, not a mime.

# Christ With You

Take Christ with you where ere you go,
Having Him there helps you to grow.
Each step you take, He knows the way
Easily guides so you won't stray.
Upheld by Him strengthens your grip
Committed to Christ is a good trip.
Harkening unto His sweet voice
Ables you to make a good choice.
Riding the wave of His presence
Instills in you great confidence.
Seek His help in all you do
Taking His advice sees you through.

# Rescuer

Ready to catch me when I fall,
Ever attentive to my call,
Dying for me upon the cross,
Erasing away all my dross,
Encouraging each step I take,
Mediating then for my sake,
Ever answering all my prayers,
Rescuer loves me and He cares.

(Written while attending the Kairos Board Meeting
in Orlando, FL)

## Ask, Seek, Knock

Ask, I was told, and I would be given
All that my heart desired.
So I asked for things, for pleasure, for
goods
Such that my state be admired.

Seek, I was told, and I would find
Such things as wisdom and power.
Knowingly I sought the things of life,
Kicking my way up the tower.

Knock, I was told, and it would be
opened –
Knowledge untold to find.
Aggressively I pounded on that door,
Attempting to improve my mind.

I had arrived, or so I thought,
Arrived at the top of the hill.
Surveying my life from that vantage
    point
Kept me wondering still.

Asking again with a yearning heart,
Alert to the leading of God,
Settled my wandering spirit down,
Safe on His path to trod.

Seeking his way in all that I do,
Staying in His tender care.
Kneeling my life before him now
Knits us together to share.

Knocking now upon His word.
Kernels of life appear.
Applying them daily as my guide
Assures me that He is near.

I am totally yielded to Him.,
Allowing Him my life to mold.
Settled on Him for all my need
Keeps me safe in His fold.

(Based on Mathew 7:7)

# Trinity

There is one God in heaven above.
He alone is whom we all should love.
Eternal life He will freely give
To whosoever His life will live.
Rejoice in Him, ever sing His praise.
Intone your voices in hymns to raise.
Unite with those who on Him do call,
Numbering yourself among His all.
Expecting your life to be anew,
Giving praise to Him in all you do.
Obey His Word in every deed,
Doing His will is all that you need.

# Ecclesia

Putting Christ as my life's center call,
Realizing that He is my all in all,
Investing my life into His way,
Enables me to endure each day.
Sharing with those who belong to Him
too,
Ties us together in all that we do.
Helping each other and reaching out
Opens our heart and makes us to shout.
Our Lord does reign and helps us to
grow,
Deepening the way our love does flow.

# Guidance

Overly cautious we can be,
Managing life for all to see.
Nearing perfection we'll not make,
Instead our own path we do take.
Seeking good guidance from above,
Control is from the heav'nly Dove.
In the image of Christ we stand
Enabled by His great command.
Now through eternity we live,
To the Christ, our life we do give.

# Jesus

Joy's an expression of His love.
Justice He brings with righteousness.
Judgment He issues with mercy.
Justifies all with tenderness.

Eternal life He freely gives.
Encouragement He e'er does bring.
Exhortation does guide our life.
Emmanuel makes my heart sing.

Stain removal is His forte.
Salvation by Him freely flows.
Substitution brought atonement.
Strength He provides gives life's
glows.

Unmerited grace He does pour.
Undeserving is what we are.
Understanding comes from His heart.
Unification He does share.

Sin forgiving is what He does.
Sovereign over all my life.
Surety against Satan’s darts.
Savior releases me from strife.

# Renewal

Leaving the vagaries of daily life
And relaxing from its toil and strife,
Knowing my spirit He will renew
Each moment I'm in this place's
milieu.
Journeying on in this faith walk so
grand,
Uniting me closer to God's own hand,
Nudging me on to a deeper faith,
Acknowledging God as my source and
light,
Learning from Him to handle all plight.
Until that day I'm in His abode
Serving Him is my life's one road.
Keeping on with His help and power,
And on Him the glory to shower.

(Based on an idea from the Prayer and Bible Conference held at Lake Junaluska, North Carolina)

# Double-Entendre

Extracted from the sands of time,
Nervous but yet without a whine,
Drilling deep for the more sublime
Orally then to have a shine.
Deeper heraldry then is sought
Openly to put on display.
Numbness sometimes is what is
brought
Tingling us with much disarray.
Inert indeed we find the line
Capping off the heraldic way.

(Written for my friend's 50th birthday party)

# God's Son

Judgement will be His alone.
Everyone before His throne
Speaking of what each has done,
Utterly without a plea
Since He gave His life for me.
Caring through eternity,
Handing me this gift so free,
Reserves me with Him to be,
In such heinous pain He strove,
Sent from God in heav'n above,
To save us through perfect love.

## Early Blessings

Persistently He seeks to draw us near,
Reaching out to us with His arms so
dear
Even though we feel no need for His
cheer.
Voicing His love in a gentle way,
Eagerly waiting for us to say
Now is the time, and this is the day.
In having that freedom to do our thing
Each day we look for some fancy new
fling
Needing, yet not knowing just how to
cling.
Tenderly He waits our change in heart,
Guarding our paths as hither we dart,
Ready to give a new life to start.
Accepting us now, reaching from
above,
Christ is patiently waiting for our love,
E'en our freedom through His heavenly
Dove.

# A Better Day

Yearning for a much better life,
Making change to reduce strife,
Choosing an ideal, not a dream,
Advancing now under full steam.

Yielding to a higher power,
Meeting with Him, my strong tower,
Claiming Him as my one strong source,
Abiding in His prescribed course.

Yes is my answer to His call,
Moving closer so I don't fall,
Capitulating to His way
Always makes for a better day.

(Written at the Donelson-Hermitage YMCÅ)

# The Trinity

Formed the earth by His own Word,
Admired what He saw and heard.
Thought about the life of man –
Had for them salvation's plan.
Eternity's His alone,
Reigns supreme upon His throne.

Set aside His deity,
Offered Himself, now I'm free;
Now He lives eternally.

Sent to help us on our way,
Paraclete for day to day.
Intercedes for us above
Raising prayers out of His love.
Indwells each who call Him in,
There helps keep us from a sin.

# His Ways

Our abundance comes from the Lord,
Managed through His amazing Word.
Newness He ever does provide,
Invites us to stay at His side.
Prepares for us our daily bread,
Refreshes us by what we're fed,
Enlivens us by what He's said.
Seeks to ever improve our way,
Entices us back when we stray.
Nudges us upward in our walk,
Takes time for us so we can talk.

# God's Goal

Marching around Jericho's wall,
Yearning to see those rocks to fall,
Starting the conquest of the land,
Advancing what the Lord had planned.
Viewing all that's before our eyes
Increases our pending surprise.
Our response is to onward plod,
Reaching for the goal set by God.

# Relying On Christ

Each day Christ does speak to our
heart,
Validating He'll not depart.
Anchored strongly in His great grace
Nuances the trials we face.
Guarded by His Holy Spirit
Expands our own spirits fit,
Leading us to greater efforts
Insuring we give good reports.
Standing firm in confrontation
Makes us strong in expectation.

## Presence of Christ

Living in the aura of Christ,
Intention of leaning on Him.
Strengthened by His words and His
grace.
Then my cup He fills to the brim.
Exciting times then I do face.
Never from Him I want to leave
I find with Him my life is trim.
Nestling in His strong embrace
Gives me comfort where ere I swim.

# Follow Christ

Believe is the beginning step,
Excitement will be very strong.
Nearness will strangely warm your
heart,
Even when you do sing a song.
Desiring Christ will give you pep,
Inclusion will bring you great peace.
Christ will ever be at your side,
The Spirit will teach what you need.
Unbind your heart, let Christ abide,
Stirrings in your heart will not cease.

# Helps

Abiding in love drives our helps,
Christ's love is the sustaining force.
Managing our helps is a gift
Yielding to our heavenly source.

Anticipating others needs
Challenges all our resources,
Moving us to great dependence,
Yet providing inner graces.

Accepting the leading of Christ
Carries our efforts up higher,
Making us stronger in our helps,
Yearning to be even better.

# God’s Gifts

Lord, keep me on Your path of love
Lest I would ever go astray.
Let me share Your love with others,
Leaning on You throughout the day.

Open Your arms, enfold me ,
Overwhelm my wandering heart.
Obeying You is my desire,
Only You can give a fresh start.

Value in life You give to us.,
Vying with You’s no game to play.
Venerate You, e’er we should do,
Voicing Your love e’en while we play.

Ever to You we owe our life,
Each day we have’s a gift from You.
Embolden us to share Your love,
Eternally You’ll see us through.

(Written at the Donelson-Hermitage YMCA)

# The Prize

It's not the swiftness of your trek,
It is the slow and steady pace
That gets you to the finish line
With a sweet smile upon your face.

Perseverance will get you through
The hills and vales of your life's way.
One other thing that you will need
Is consistence in prayer each day.

Prayer's the foundation of each day
Upon which to build as you rise.
Remember that in all you do
Eternal life with Christ's the prize.

(Written at the Donelson-Hermitage YMCA)

# Renewal

Hope springs eternal in our soul,
An adornment that brings life.
Perseverance must then ensue,
Passivity will bring us strife.
Yielding to the Spirit's leading
Nourishes our spirit to grow,
Enhancing our zest for life,
Wringing contentment that will show.
Yearning for continuation
Encourages us to take part.
Advancing our desire to see
Renewal for our wand'ring heart.

# Abide In Christ

Abiding in Christ is not free,
Strength and perseverance required.
Helping others also helps us,
Energizing us though we're tired.
Seeking God's help for our neighbor
Teaches us about compassion,
Overriding innate shyness
And giving us a new passion.
Steadfastness in our walk with Christ
Helps us thus to follow His lead.
Eagerly we labor for Him
Serve others' how us He does feed.

# Helper

Teaching through each moment of life,
Heeding to do God's perfect will.
Eager to help in any way,
Holding God's mandate to fulfill.
Obedience is the best way,
Looking to help what e'er the cost.
Yielding ever to God's leading,
Seeking to save all that are lost.
Pleading on behalf of each one,
Inviting all to grow in God.
Remember God is in control,
Including each step that you plod.
Taking time so your head wont nod.

# Growth in Christ

Prayer prepares you for renewal,
Remembering God's in control.
Always let God do the leading,
Yes, Him only we should extol.
Establish your own quiet time
Reserving a place with Him to meet
And let it be your sacred place
Nudge you to bow at Jesus' feet.
Discipline helps you to be true,
Fasting's also a discipline,
Adding depth to your love of Christ,
Seeking the Christ above life's din.
Tenacious in your discipline
Instills a desire for the Lord.
Newness in life always comes by
Growing daily in the Lord's Word.

# Life With God

Adorn yourself with the attire of God.
Remember the things God wants you to
do.
Make room in your day to receive
God's blog.
Open your Bible and keep the dust off.
Rejoice in the Lord, make it your
motto.
Open your arms with a hug to offer.
Forgive and you'll receive forgiveness
too.
Give of yourself and you'll be
someone's dream.
Obeisance makes you rich in faith, not
poor.
Defer to the Lord, for He is your Abba.

(This poem is a double acrostic.
Read down the first letter of each line
and read up the last letter of each line.)

# God's Love

Giving your all throughout this day,
Ordered by the way that you pray,
Determines the result you get,
Strengthens your desire not to fret.
Staying with the plan that's been giv'n
Opens the way that leads to heav'n.
Now that you have the goal in mind
Intentionality will bind
Several steps to reach your goal,
Reminding you God's in control.
Inviting God to show His way
Sustains that path so you won't stray,
Enabling you to meet the task,
Nudging you in God's love to bask.

(Written at the Donelson-Hermitage YMCA)

# Extol Christ

Animosity's sneaking in,
Making life a but tough to live.
Anxiety's taking a toll,
Zooming in on how much to give.
Inklings of Christ come to the fore,
Numbing anxiety's effect.
Gaining confidence in the Lord,
Grace's sprinklings you can detect.
Racing wildly into Christ's arms,
Aching to have Christ in control,
Chasing away all doubt and fear,
Enthralled that Christ I can extol.

# The Christ

Putting our hearts and minds to work
Enab'ling God's Spirit to shine.
Releasing our being to God
So at His table we can dine.
Exhibiting Christ in our life,
Valuing Christ and what He has done,
Ever thankful that God saved us,
Recall eternal life He's won.
Adoration we ere do bring
Naming Christ as the Holy One.
Conviction shows that in our life
Exalting Christ, God's only Son.

(Written at Grace Place Church)

# Servants

Filling my life with so much joy,
Reaching out with helps to offer.
In deep reverence with the Lord
Entreating with much time in prayer.
Never shirking God's sacred Word,
Desiring to be His servant,
Seeking times to serve, not be heard.

(Written at Grace Place Church)

# Christ's Actions

Rescued by Christ from the pit's strong
glove,
Eagerly sought through Christ's
gracious love.
Desolation was all I did face,
Embraced by Christ through amazing
grace.
Empty was the extent of my stance,
Mercy the Christ laved in abundance.
Equipped by Christ I did not despise,
Dwelling with Christ the ultimate prize.

(Written at the home of Kathy and Tom Gilmore in New Palestine, IN)

# Your Life

Just believing is not enough,
Easy is not a way to live,
Show action by what you give.
Underestimate takes your breath,
Shows you have a lack of breadth.
Instinct is a life that is tough.
Sloth in every form is sin,
Leads you to society's din.
Order your life to be with God
Reaping true life where e'er you trod.
Denial will keep you in the rough.

# Lenten Growth

Letting go of some special things,
Eager for the coming event,
Neat new insights are gleaned each day
Trekking toward the end of Lent.

Learning more about inner self
Enables us to ever grow
Nearer to such a unique plan
That the Christ on us will bestow.

Loving Christ in a deeper way
Enhances the life that we live.
Now we can more appreciate
The sacrifice that Christ did give.

# In His Arms

Yearning for the presence of God,
Making time for His Word to read,
Changing my ways to fit His plan
And ever yielding to His lead.

Yesterday my life He did lead
Making things ready for today,
Crafting His plan for betterment,
Assessing progress to His way.

Yielding to His Spirit's guiding
Makes me a disciple that's strong.
Choosing His way is always best
And in His arms' where I belong.

(Written at the Donelson-Hermitage YMCA)

# Now

Pushing things for later to do
Rather than doing it while it's new,
Only more clutter for your life,
Changing your way would be less
strife.
Realizing you need to persevere,
Acting now when issues appear
So they don't put you in a stew
Today and now start ways anew.
Inviting yourself to move on
Nudging you each moment of dawn.
Asking Christ's help is what you do
To change now for a better you.
Investing in time with the Lord
Open your life to hear God's Word,
Now praise God whenever it's due.

# Believe

Gifts from God we earnestly seek,
Realizing we have no control
As we do wait, we should be meek,
Centered on God whom we extol,
Eager we work to that high peak.

Guidance from God we ever need,
Including patience for our heart.
Valuing all that He does feed,
Enriching our life, ev'ry part,
Sowing His Word like we do seed.

Personal growth we do receive
Each time we go to God in prayer.
And understanding we achieve,
Causing us to want to share,
Establishing why we believe.

# Preparation

Come gracious Lord and calm my
 mind,
Only in You, solace I find.
Meld me into Your perfect way,
Energizing me for the day.

Hold me firmly within Your heart,
Organizing this day to start.
Lave my being so I'll be clean,
Yielding, so in me Christ is seen.

Sequester all my mind and soul,
Paving the way for Your control.
Inhabit every part of me,
Reminding me in You I'm free.
Inspiring me to persevere,
Teaching me in You there's no fear.

(Written at the Donelson-Hermitage YMCA)

# God's Leadings

You are the rock on which I stand,
You are the cleft where I can hide.
You are the source for all my life,
Making You to be my life's guide.

Meeting discipline without dread,
Making fulfillment of my need.
Claiming me as one of Your own,
Clarifying Your Word as I read.

Calming my spirit, soul and heart,
Always there to show me Your way.
Abundantly blessings my life,
Advising me on how to pray.

# God

Setting the pace for the new day,
Owning events and then to pray,
Umbrage we take along the way,
Listening to what God does say.

Being present for each moment,
Organized so there's no lament.
Doing without making a comment,
Yearning to hear God's compliment.

Making the space for God's leading,
Intentional without pleading.
Needing God's love and His feeding
Doing God's will without bleating.

(Written at the Donelson-Hermitage YMCA)

# Ask

Abundant life there is to live,
Acknowledging Christ as the source.
Aligning with Christ's full control,
Accepting His way and His course.

Seeking forever Christ to serve,
Stepping forth in His guiding love.
Seeing Christ as fullness in God,
Standing on the words from the Dove.

Knees bent to show adoration,
Keeping Christ as our center thought.
Kingdom vision is our focus,
Key: that the Christ our soul has
bought.

(Written at the Donelson-Hermitage YMCA)

## Surrender

Graciousness is a way of life.
Invitational's an asset.
Vitality enlivens you,
Establishes you aren't done yet.
Temper your efforts on each day
Hieing to follow the Christ's way.
As you step forth along God's path,
Nearer to Him you strive to be,
Knowing full well you need His help,
Surrender to Him is the key.

# Change

As we do advance through the years,
Changes occur that may bring tears.
Riding along with each new change
Orients life to a new range.
Stepping up into a new way
Tends to lead to more time to pray,
Indicates we still can comply,
Choosing Christ is our reason why.

# Other Books of Poems By the Author

2023

2023

2023

2024

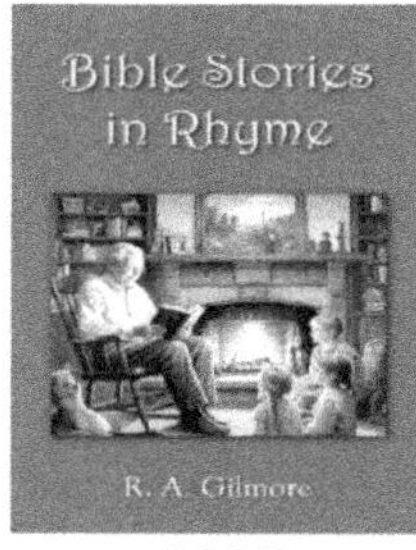

2025

2025

2012
[out of print]

2019
[get from author]

2020 – PDF
[get from author]

www.ingramcontent.com/pod-product-compliance
Lightning Source LLC
LaVergne TN
LVHW020656100826
845148LV00012B/2515

* 9 7 9 8 9 8 7 2 7 6 6 6 2 *